Transportation

Ships

by Mari Schuh

CAPSTONE PRESS
a capstone imprint

Little Pebble is published by Capstone Press,
1710 Roe Crest Drive, North Mankato, Minnesota 56003
www.mycapstone.com

Library of Congress Cataloging-in-Publication Data
Names: Schuh, Mari C., 1975- author.
Title: Ships / by Mari Schuh.
Description: North Mankato, Minnesota : Capstone Press, [2017] | Series:
    Little pebble. Transportation | "Little Pebble is published by
    Capstone Press." | Audience: Ages 4-8. | Audience: K to grade 3. | Includes
    bibliographical references and index.
Identifiers: LCCN 2016059070
    ISBN 978-1-5157-7301-6 (library binding)
    ISBN 978-1-5157-7307-8 (paperback)
    ISBN 978-1-5157-7313-9 (ebook pdf)
Subjects: LCSH: Ships—Juvenile literature.
Classification: LCC VM150 .S338 2018 | DDC 623.8—dc23
LC record available at https://lccn.loc.gov/2016059070

Editorial Credits
Carrie Braulick Sheely, editor; Lori Bye, designer; Wanda Winch, media researcher;
Katy LaVigne, production specialist

Photo Credits
Dreamstime: Jordanker, 11; Shutterstock: Alex Kolokythas Photography, 21, Alvov, cover, 13, amophoto_
au, 15, donvictorio, 7, Eastimages, 9, Igor Karasi, 17, Ivan Cholakov, 5, T. Sumaetho, zoom motion
design; U.S. Navy Photo by Petty Officer 3rd Class Nathan T. Beard, 19

Printed and bound in China.
010429F17

Table of Contents

At Sea

A ship sails by.

People wave.

Hello!

Parts

Look at the big engine.

It makes power.

engine

Look at the propeller.

The engine makes it spin.

Then the ship moves.

propeller

Look at the rudder.

It helps steer the ship.

rudder

This ship has sails.

Sails use the wind to move the ship.

Kinds

Look at the cruise ship.

It is full of people.

They have fun!

A tanker is full of liquid.

It carries tons of oil.

Here is an aircraft carrier.

It carries warplanes.

Time for takeoff!

Here is a cargo ship.

It carries big boxes.

What might be inside?

Glossary

aircraft carrier—a warship with a large, flat deck where aircraft take off and land

cargo ship—a ship that carries large amounts of goods

cruise ship—a large ship that people travel on for vacations

engine—a machine that makes the power needed to move something

propeller—a set of rotating blades; a propeller makes the force to move a ship through water

rudder—a flat metal piece attached to a ship that is used for steering

sail—a large sheet of strong cloth on a ship; a sail catches the wind to move the ship

tanker—a ship with tanks that carries large amounts of liquid

Read More

Adamson, Thomas. *Ships*. Minneapolis: Bellwether Media, 2017.

Meister, Cari. *Ships.* Bullfrog Books: Machines at Work. Minneapolis, Minn.: Jump!, 2014.

Veitch, Catherine. *Big Machines Float!* Big Machines. Chicago: Heinemann Library, 2015.

Internet Sites

Use FactHound to find Internet sites related to this book.

Visit *www.facthound.com*

Just type in 9781515773016 and go.

 Super-cool stuff!

Check out projects, games and lots more at
www.capstonekids.com

Critical Thinking Questions

1. What parts help ships move through the water?

2. Why are ships good at transporting items?

3. Use another book or a website to learn about boats. How are ships different from boats? How are they the same?

Index